THE READING
DRUMMER

Rhythms, Rolls, Flams, Ruffs, and More!

A Logical Step-by-Step Sequence of Rhythms and Drumming

This book contains lessons for learning to read drum music.

The author has spent many years researching how students progress as they learn and develop their reading and technical proficiency. The graphic presentations, phrasing logic, and physical coordination used in this book reflect this research and experience.

The book is ideal for students as they first begin drum lessons or for drummers interested in learning how to read music.

Upon completion of this book, the student should be well on his way to becoming a fine percussionist with a thorough understanding of the fundamental rhythms that a drummer will encounter.

3RD EDITION COMPLETELY UPDATED & REVISED

Dave Vose

Berklee Press

Vice President: Dave Kusek
Dean of Continuing Education: Debbie Cavalier
Managing Editor: Jonathan Feist
Director of Business Affairs: Robert F. Green
Senior Designer: Robert Heath

ISBN-13: 978-0-634-00961-7

Berklee Press

1140 Boylston Street
Boston, MA 02215-3693 USA
(617) 747-2146

Visit Berklee Press Online at
www.berkleepress.com

DISTRIBUTED BY

HAL•LEONARD® CORPORATION
7777 W. BLUEMOUND RD. P.O. BOX 13819
MILWAUKEE, WISCONSIN 53213

Visit Hal Leonard Online at
www.halleonard.com

THE READING
DRUMMER

CONTENTS

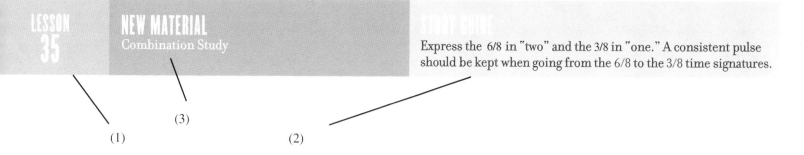

LESSON
35

NEW MATERIAL
Combination Study

STUDY GUIDE

Express the 6/8 in "two" and the 3/8 in "one." A consistent pulse
should be kept when going from the 6/8 to the 3/8 time signatures.

(1)   (3)

(2)

HOW TO USE THIS BOOK

Each lesson introduces either a new concept or a Combination Study of materials previously
learned. It is important that the student masters each lesson before moving on to the next.

Each lesson is numbered (1) for easy reference and includes a "Study Guide" (2) that will be
helpful for the student to receive the maximum benefit from the materials presented on the
page. "New Material" (3) is indicated at the top of each page.

At first, it may be difficult to do an entire lesson every week. If so, a portion of the lesson
(one-half or one-third of the lesson) may be more suitable, especially if the student is also
practicing other material. The pages labeled *Combination Study* should be done as a
complete composition.

Metronome markings are not given (except for Lessons 47, 49, and 50) so that the lesson can be
practiced at a variety of tempos. A teacher can also assign a specific metronome marking if he
wishes. The ability to perform with a steady tempo and with accurate performance of the rhythms
is, of course, very important.

Specific stickings are not included so that each teacher can use his own method of teaching them
(except for Lessons 48–50).

Dynamic markings and *articulations* should be carefully observed so that the student's
musicianship will improve along with his reading and playing ability. When dynamics are not
indicated, they can be written in by the teacher, if so desired.

It is recommended that when the student is approaching a lesson that contains *a new drumming
technique* that may be difficult (e.g., rolls, flams, etc.), the teacher should prepare the student for
it before reaching the lesson. For example, flams are introduced as new material in lesson 34. By
that time, the student should have been taught how to play a flam.

Duets, after each set of ten lessons, are a wonderful way to develop accuracy, balance, and
concentration.

INSTRUMENTATION

Some of these exercises can be practiced on a drum set, as well as a single instrument. Here are some ways to use them with a drum set.

1. Hi-hat, right hand, play steady eighth notes.
2. Snare drum, left hand, play the written line.
3. Bass drum, play steady quarter notes.

Here's how line 1 from lesson 10 would work on a drum set.

Another approach:
1. Ride cymbal, right hand, play steady eighth notes.
2. Snare drum, left hand, play only eighth notes in the written line.
3. Bass drum, play notes in the written line that are a quarter note or longer.

Also, try writing your own original patterns. Here is line 3 from lesson 10 in the snare, with new parts written for bass drum and hi-hat.

There are many other ways to use these exercises on drum set. Use your imagination, and enjoy the process.

NEW MATERIAL

Quarter Notes and Quarter Rests

STUDY GUIDE

Counting out loud will help you to understand the time signature.

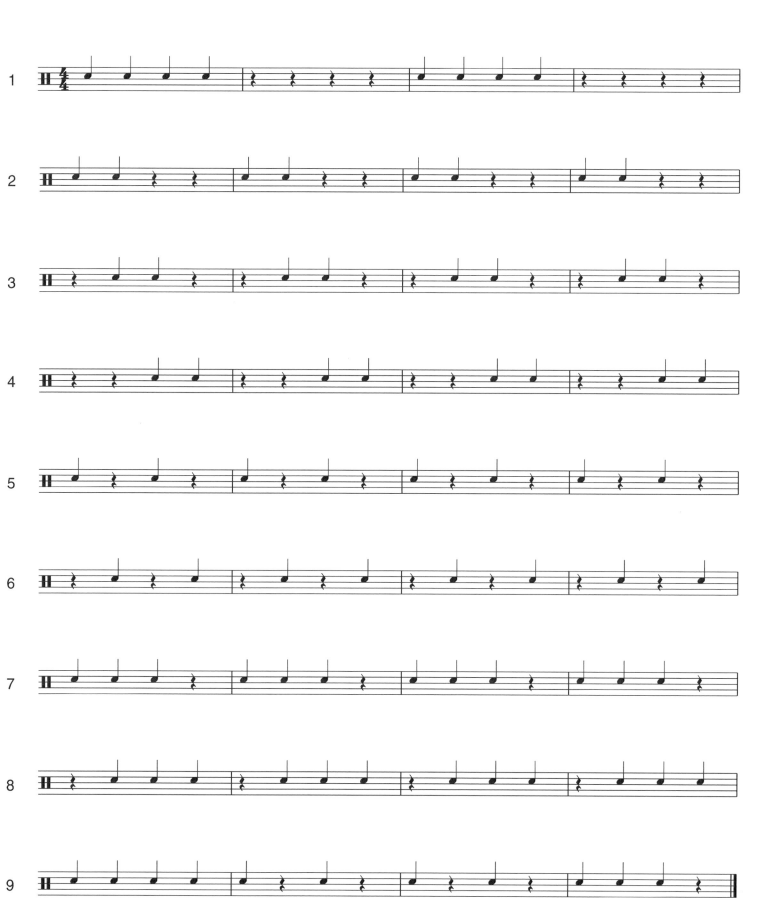

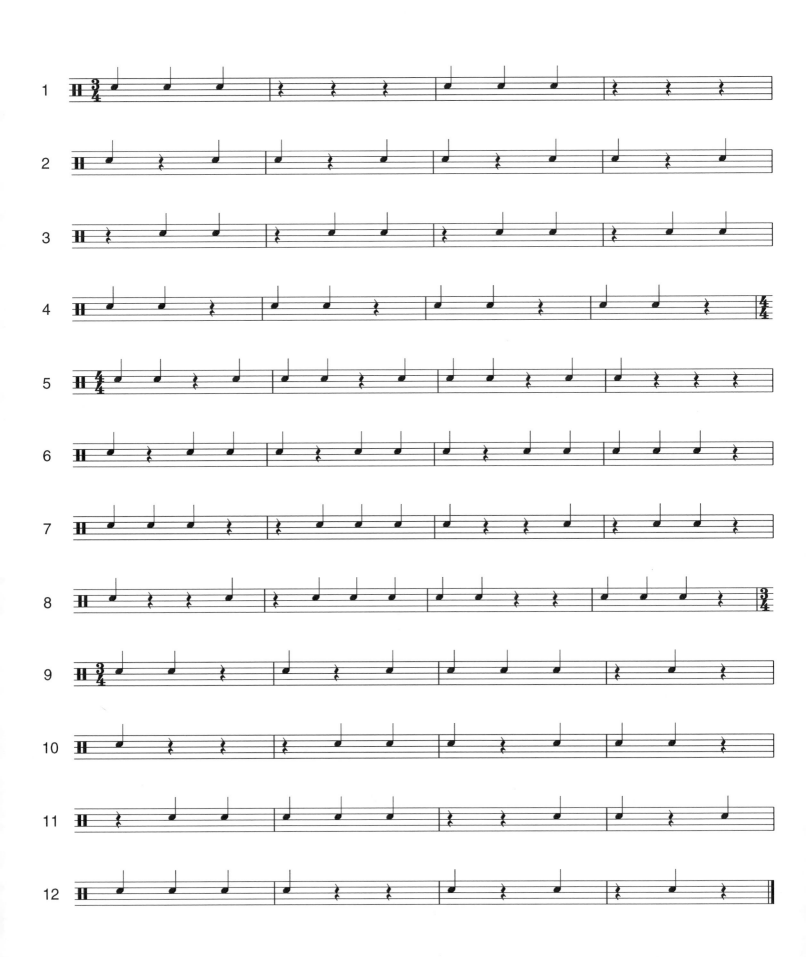

LESSON 3

NEW MATERIAL
♪ Eighth Notes

STUDY GUIDE
Count the upbeat eighth notes by saying "and."

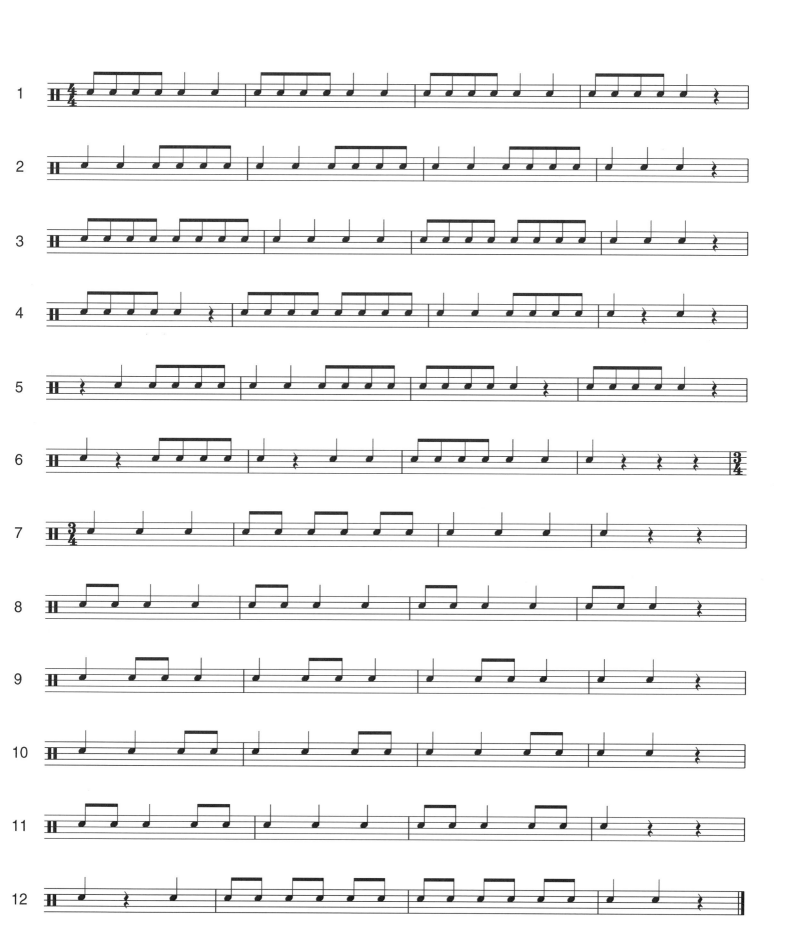

LESSON 4

NEW MATERIAL
Combination Study

STUDY GUIDE
Strive for a balanced sound between your right-hand stroke and left-hand stroke.

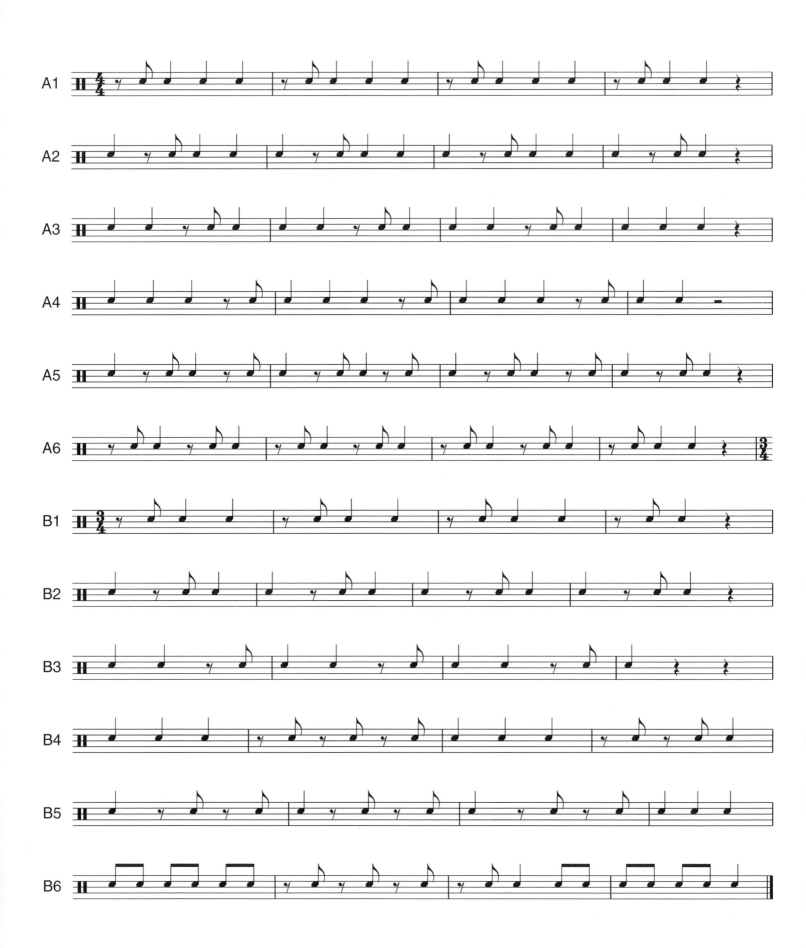

A1

A2

A3

B1

B2

B3

C1

C2

C3

D1

D2

D3

LESSON 8

NEW MATERIAL
Ties

STUDY GUIDE
Although a snare drum note does not sustain, imagine the sound of the sustained tied note.

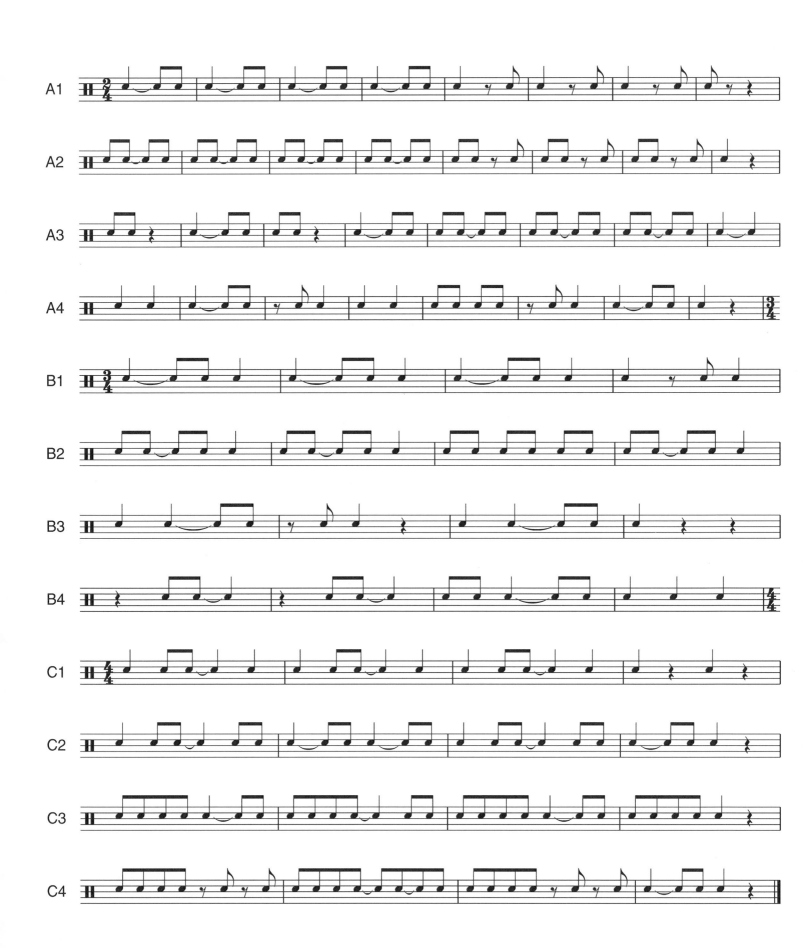

NEW MATERIAL

Dots ·

A dot increases the note by half its value. A quarter note therefore receives 1½ beats of value in 2/4, 3/4, or 4/4.

LESSON 10

NEW MATERIAL
Combination Study

STUDY GUIDE
Keep a steady tempo when playing from line to line and from time signature to time signature.

STUDY GUIDE

When performing a duet, rhythmic accuracy is essential. Recording the performance is a good way to confirm that unison parts are performed precisely together and that the rhythmic interplay between parts is accurate.

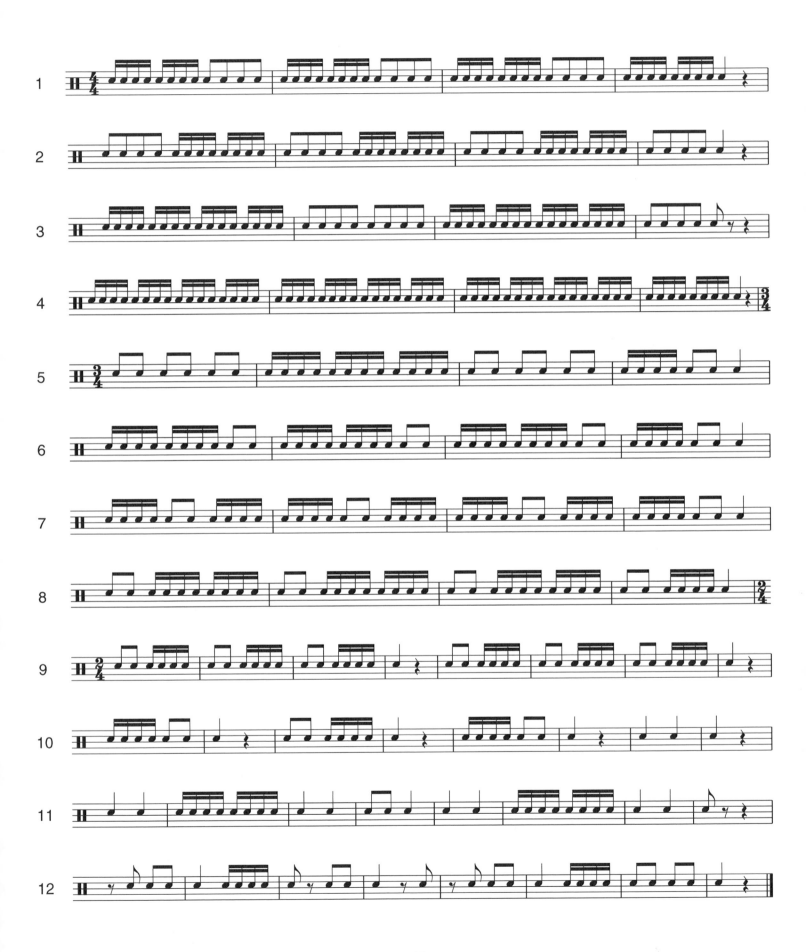

LESSON 12

NEW MATERIAL
Abbreviation for Four Sixteenth Notes

STUDY GUIDE
Use a metronome and practice a variety of tempos.

NEW MATERIAL
♪♪♪ Pattern

STUDY GUIDE
Develop your stroke sensitivity by practicing a variety of dynamic levels.

NEW MATERIAL

♪♪♪ Pattern

NEW MATERIAL
Eighth-Note Triplets

STUDY GUIDE
Space the triplet notes evenly.

18

LESSON
18

NEW MATERIAL
Combination Study

STUDY GUIDE
Keep a steady pulse while changing time signatures.

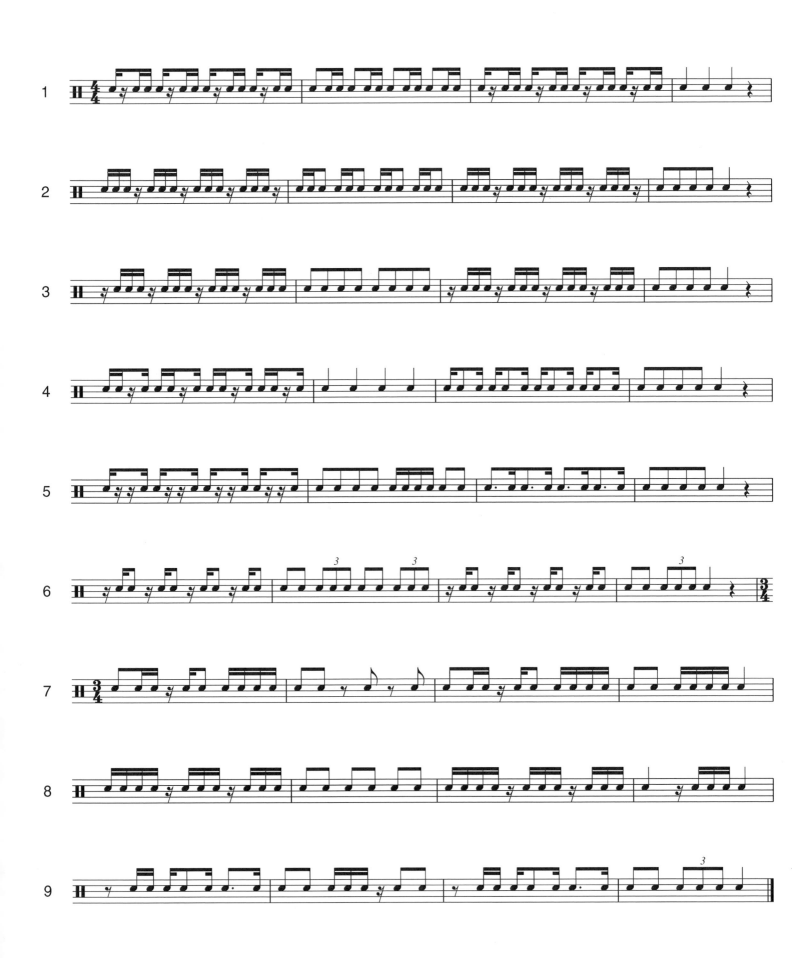

STUDY GUIDE
Determine the most appropriate tempo for this duet.

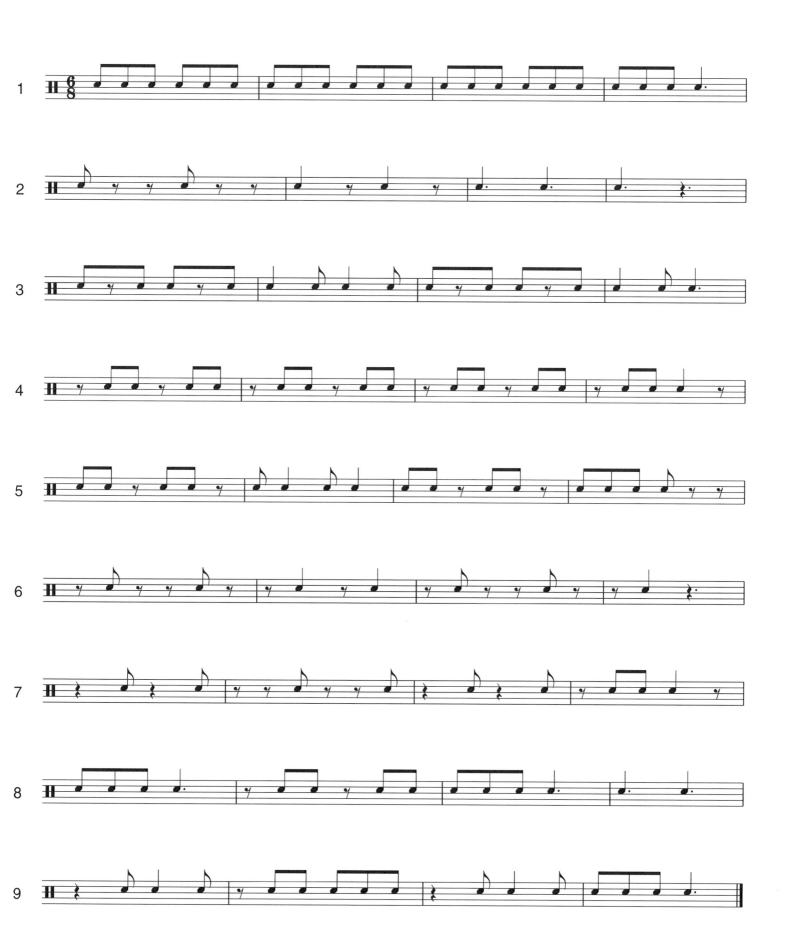

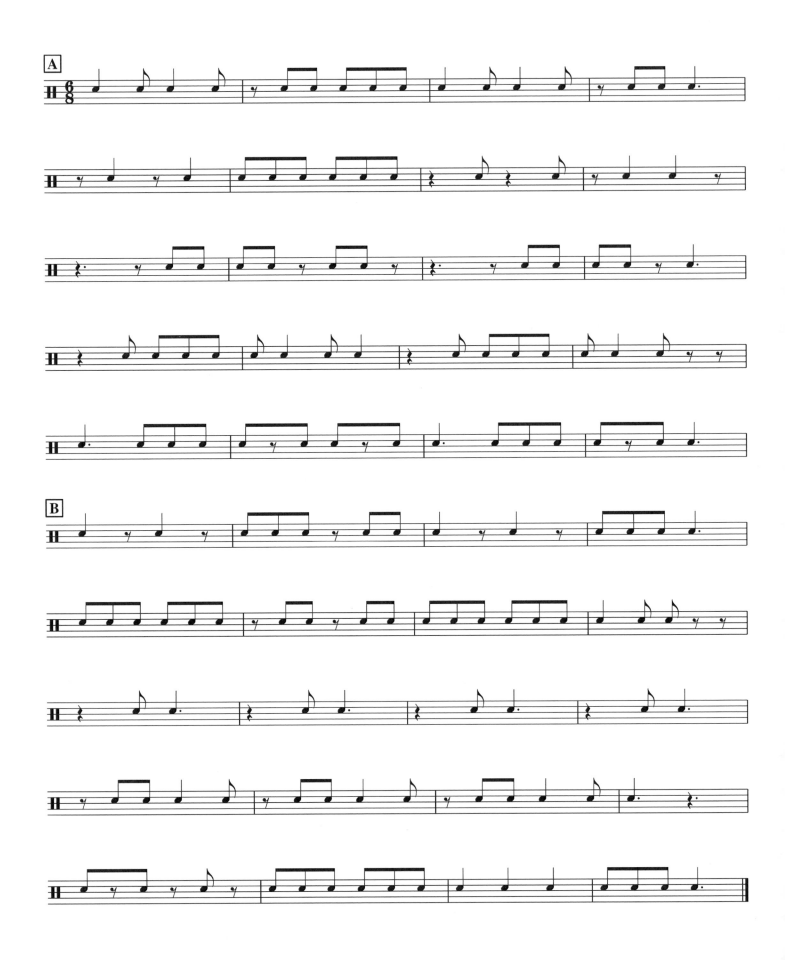

LESSON 24

NEW MATERIAL
Cut Time/Alla Breve

STUDY GUIDE
Cut time is felt in "2." A half note gets one beat.

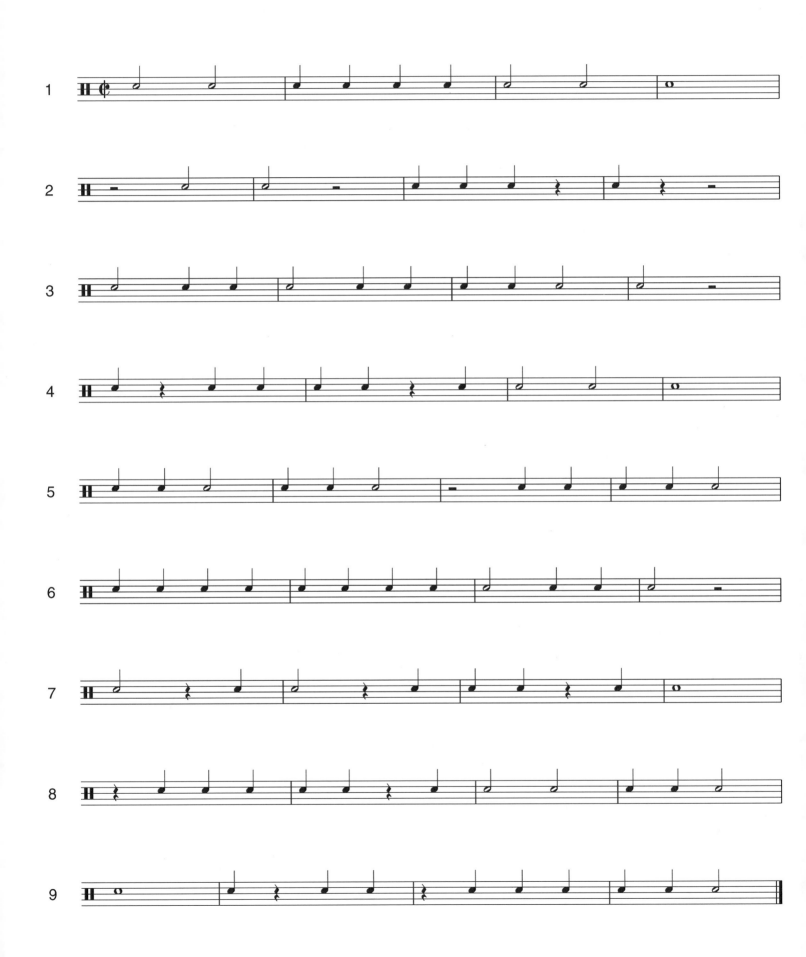

LESSON
26

NEW MATERIAL
Rolls

STUDY GUIDE
Strive for a good quality roll sound and maintain a
consistent tempo throughout the duration of the roll.

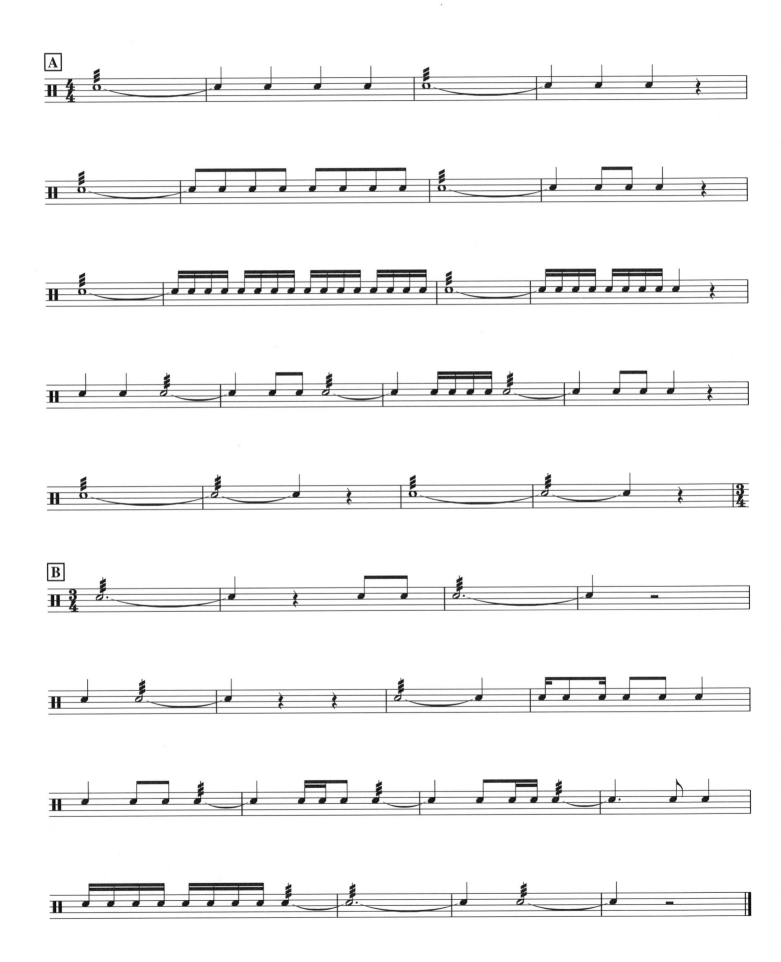

NEW MATERIAL
Short Rolls

LESSON 29

NEW MATERIAL
6/8 Rolls

STUDY GUIDE
Double the sixteenth-note strokes to create the roll as shown in measure 2.

LESSON 30

NEW MATERIAL
Sixteenth Rests in 6/8 Time

STUDY GUIDE
Snare drum music is sometimes notated with
the stems going down.

STUDY GUIDE

Do not start this duet too quickly because the music becomes increasingly active at measure 5.

LESSON 35

NEW MATERIAL
Combination Study

STUDY GUIDE
Express the 6/8 in "two" and the 3/8 in "one." A consistent pulse
should be kept when going from the 6/8 to the 3/8 time signatures.

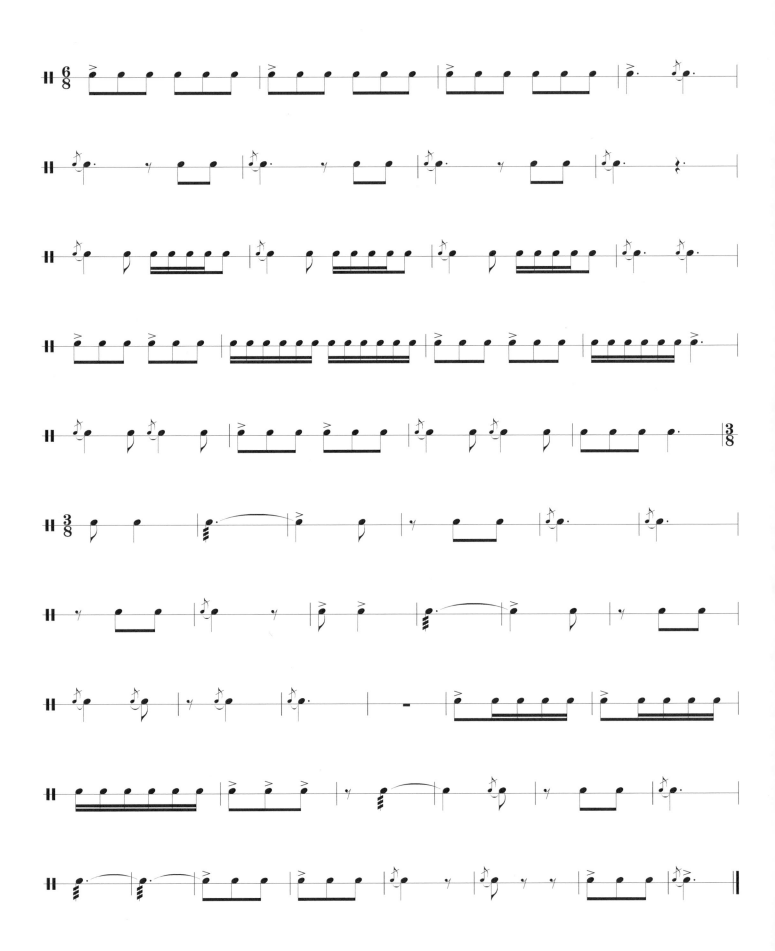

LESSON
36

NEW MATERIAL
Dynamics

STUDY GUIDE
The observance of dynamics is important for developing musicality. A slash through the note stem means to play two notes.

LESSON 37

NEW MATERIAL
Sixteenth-Note Triplets
and Measure Repeats ✕

STUDY GUIDE
Developing good single stroke technique will help the performance of sixteenth-note triplets. The ✕ means to repeat the previous measure one time.

40

LESSON
38

NEW MATERIAL
Broken Triplets and Rim Shots

STUDY GUIDE
The rim shot is notated with an × for the notehead.
R.S. is also used.

LESSON
39
NEW MATERIAL
Changing Meters

STUDY GUIDE
Keep the eighth note consistent when changing meters.

1

2

3

4

5

6

7

8

LESSON 40

NEW MATERIAL

Fermatas ⌢ and D.C.

STUDY GUIDE

Hold the fermata until direction is given to continue. D.C. stands for Da Capo, which means to repeat the composition from the beginning.

STUDY GUIDE

Perform the notes with a ✕ notehead as a stick-on-stick rimshot. Also, blend and balance the dynamics for a complete musical performance.

✕ = Rim shot

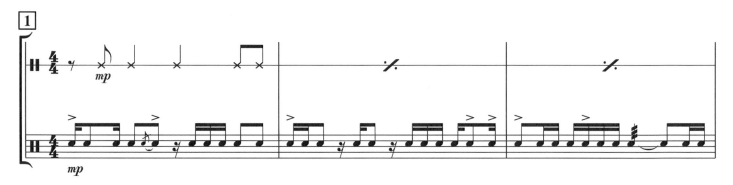

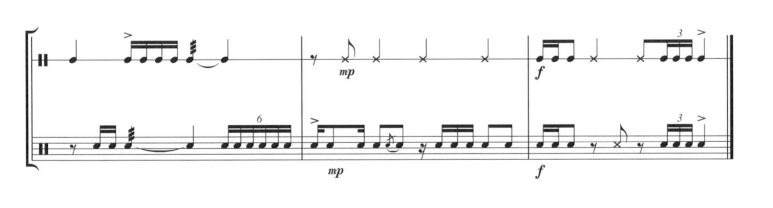

LESSON 41

NEW MATERIAL
Buzz Rolls (**z**), Tenutos (**-**), Staccatos (**•**), and Tempo Changes

STUDY GUIDE
A "**z**" is sometimes used to specify a buzz roll. Hold notes with tenuto markings their full value. Play staccato notes very short.

LESSON 42

NEW MATERIAL
Combination Study

STUDY GUIDE
Practice this lesson at a variety of tempos.

LESSON 43

NEW MATERIAL
Ruffs  and Two-Measure Repeats

STUDY GUIDE
Rebound technique is used for the performance of double grace notes. The ⁂ means to play the previous two measures one time.

LESSON 45

NEW MATERIAL
1st and 2nd Endings, Caesuras (//), and
Four-Stroke Ruffs

STUDY GUIDE
A caesura indicates a slight pause in the music. Observe proper
technique while playing this large variety of musical expressions.

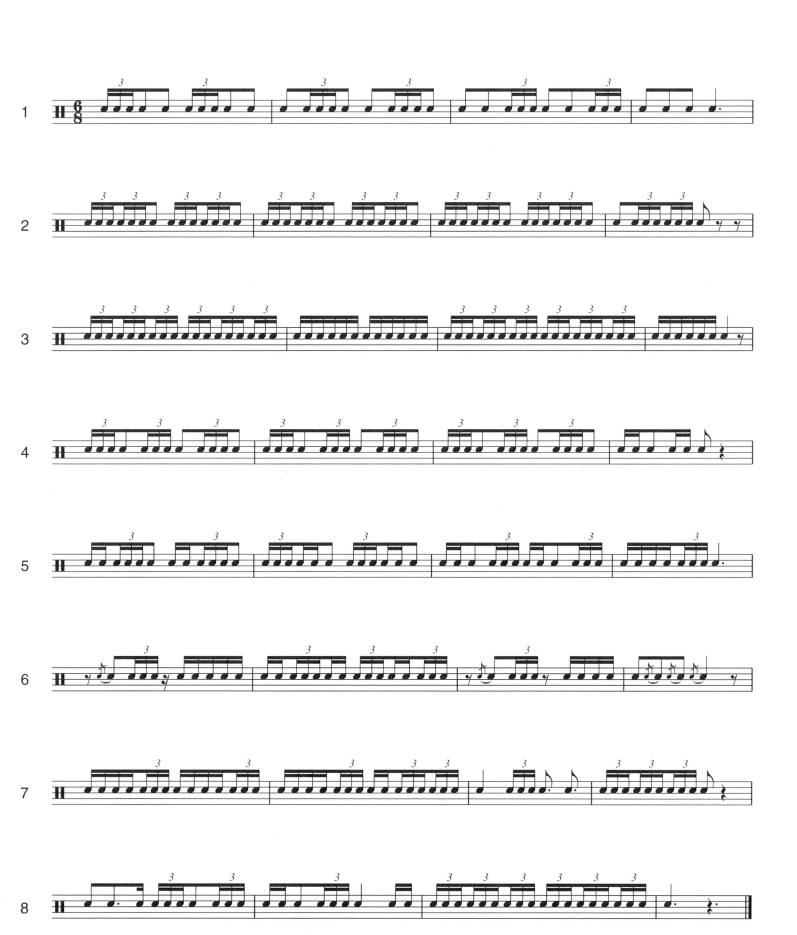

NEW MATERIAL
Combination Study

LESSON 48

NEW MATERIAL
Beam Over Bar and Stickings

STUDY GUIDE
At times, stickings are written in to aid musical expression.
Be expressive but don't sacrifice accuracy.

LESSON
49

NEW MATERIAL
12/8 Time, Dal Segno al Coda, ♪♪♪ , and
Immediate Tempo Changes

STUDY GUIDE
12/8 has four pulses per measure. Dal Segno al Coda/D.S. al Coda mean to go
to the sign, then take the CODA. Practice each tempo change separately.

LESSON 50

NEW MATERIAL
Striking the Rim, "4" over "3," and 32nd Notes.

STUDY GUIDE
Watch striking areas when moving from rim to head. The 4:3 quarters sound as dotted eighths. Keep 32nd notes even.

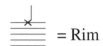 = Rim

DUET 5

STUDY GUIDE
This duet uses both orchestral-style buzz rolls ♩ and open double stroke rolls ♩.

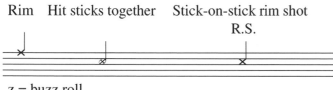

Rim   Hit sticks together   Stick-on-stick rim shot
R.S.

z = buzz roll